Jean Vanier

I walk with JESUS

Dear brother and sister,

Perhaps you have already read the first book I MEET JESUS. It speaks about meeting Jesus, the Savior, who changes our lives deeply by giving us new hope. It tells of the Good News Jesus came to bring: how He lived, how He healed the sick, how He was condemned and put to death, how He rose from the dead, how He sent His Holy Spirit and founded the Church.

This book is a follow-up to the first one. It explains more in detail how Jesus invites us to live, to follow Him, to be His disciples, His friends, today, in our world.

So often, we are like the disciples of Emmaus. Jesus is close to us, He walks with us but we do not recognize Him.

These pages were written to help us recognize Jesus, to see more clearly where He is alive and present in our world today.

The book begins with the story we all know quite well: two disciples on their way to Emmaus. After Jesus' death, they are running away from their community and from Jerusalem. They are discouraged. This is the introduction of the book!

Then, Jesus approaches them. He starts walking with them, He talks to them about the Bible. He reveals that He is the Savior, who was called to suffer a great deal in order to enter into His glory. This is the first part of the book.

So often, we too run away from suffering, our own and that of others. We do not realize that Jesus is hidden in those who suffer. He calls us to bear and offer both our pain and the suffering of others.

Then Jesus accepts the disciples' invitation. He sits down at table with them. When He takes bread, blesses it, breaks it and gives it to the disciples, they recognize Him. Yes, Jesus is present; He is hidden in the bread of the Eucharist. This is the second part of the book.

Finally, having recognized Jesus, the two disciples quickly go back to Jerusalem; they go back to the community of the disciples. Jesus is present in community: in the family community and in all the other different types of Christian communities. This is the third part.

I hope this book will help you, my brother, my sister, to recognize Jesus in your own life. Open your heart to Him. He will lead you to deep joy. He will help you know His Father. You will become a friend of the Father, the Son and the Holy Spirit. You will meet Mary, His Mother, and the whole wonderful family of God.

You will recognize Jesus, hidden in people's hearts, especially in those who are weak and broken. Thus, you will no longer be alone. With them, you will learn how to live, to give and receive more fully and you will build the Kingdom together.

Jesus has just died.
Two of His disciples are walking away
from Jerusalem and from their community.

Their hearts are in despair.
They had put all their hope in Jesus.
He was for them a truly great prophet.

But now He is dead.
Everything is finished.
Their lives are completely broken.

But Jesus is risen from the dead
and really living!

He approaches the two disciples
and starts walking with them.
They do not recognize Him.

Jesus asks them: "Why are you sad?"
One of them answers:

> "You are the only one who does not know
> what happened in Jerusalem
> these past few days!"

Then Jesus says:

> "You foolish men, so slow to believe the full
> message of the prophets.
> Was it not necessary that Christ suffer
> and thus enter into His glory?"

He then talks to them about the Bible.
He shows them that all He suffered
    had been announced by the prophets.

Luke 24, 13-35

Then, evening comes.
They arrive at a small inn near
the town of Emmaus.

Jesus pretends to go on his way.
The disciples beg Him: "Stay with us!"
He accepts.
He sits down at table with them.
He takes bread, blesses it, breaks it
and gives it to them.
When He does this, they recognize Him.
"It's Jesus," they say.

But He has vanished from their sight.
He is now present in the bread
and present in their hearts.

The two disciples say to each other:
"Did not our hearts burn within us
as He talked to us on the road?"

They return quickly to Jerusalem
in spite of the dangers that await them.
Deeper than the fear,
there is the certainty
that Jesus is present in them.
Once they are back in the community
of the disciples, they say:

"We have seen Jesus!
He is truly alive!"

Their hearts are full of joy.

Luke 24, 34

We are so like these two disciples.
So often we walk along the road of life
discouraged and full of our own problems.
We are afraid to suffer.

We are frightened to be with others who suffer.
We seek distractions; we try to forget
and to escape reality.

We want to be comfortable and secure.
We are caught up in ourselves.
We do not recognize Jesus, alive and present,
       in all those who are suffering in our world.

One day, Jesus tells this story:

A man is walking from Jerusalem to Jericho.
Some robbers attack him, knock him down
and take his money.
They leave him on the road,
                              wounded and half-dead.

Luke 10, 29-37

A priest passes by.
He sees the man on the ground
but he turns away;
he does not want to come close to him.

Another man passes by
and does the same thing.

Both of them are frightened.
They do not want to be disturbed
by this man in pain,
lying all alone on the ground.

A stranger passes by.
When he sees the man in distress,
he is deeply touched.
He is a man with a warm
and compassionate heart.
So he comes close to the wounded man,
takes him in his arms and comforts him.
He loves him.

With much kindness and gentleness
he puts him on a donkey
and takes him to the nearest inn.

There he continues to care for him.
He feeds him and spends the night with him.
The next day he tells the innkeeper:

"Please give him food
and take care of him.
I will pay you when I come back."

Jesus asks us to be like this stranger,
to have a heart full of compassion
and to comfort the afflicted.

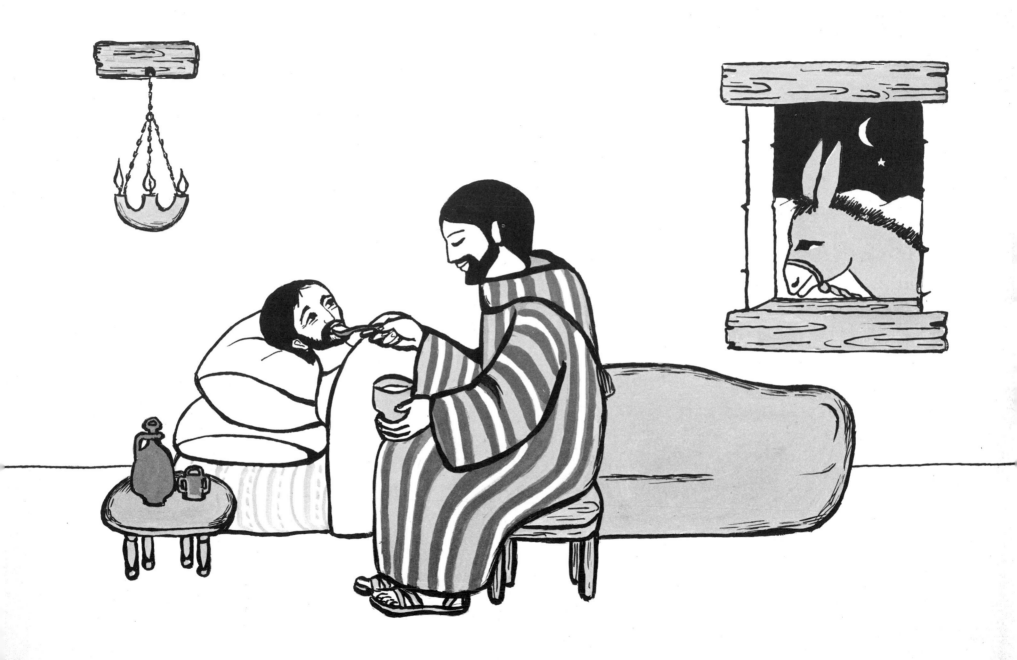

We too are frightened to come close
to people in pain.

We turn away.
We continue along the road
without looking at them.
We are too preoccupied with our own lives.
We are closed up in our own comfortable houses.
We are afraid.

We forget those who are dying of hunger.
We do not welcome children
who have been abandoned.
We close our doors to foreigners, to immigrants.
We refuse people who have a handicap.

We ignore those who are in prison
or shut up in hospitals.
We do not go and visit them.
We are afraid to enter into their prison
of sadness.

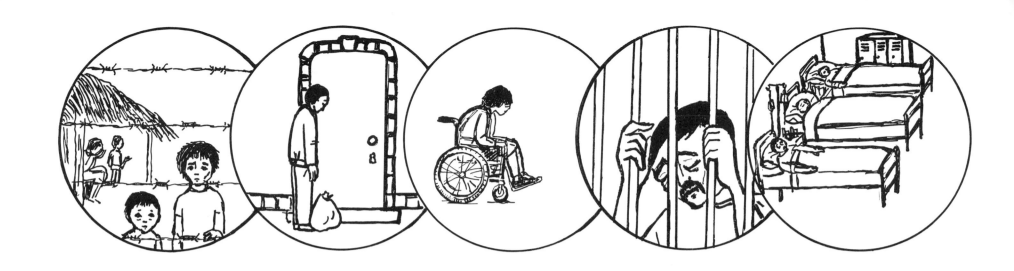

But Jesus invites us to be close to the afflicted,
to care for them,
to love them,
to discover their beauty,
to enter into relationship with them.

Jesus tells another story.

There was a man called Lazarus.
He was very poor.
He had no home but lived in the street.
He had nothing to eat.
He was covered with sores.

Nearby, there lived a very rich man.
He had a beautiful house.
There he invited his friends.
They ate, drank, danced,
and had a good time together.
They were not at all concerned
with the hungry Lazarus.
He hungered for scraps
from the rich man's table.

Luke 16, 19-30

One day, Lazarus died.
The Father immediately welcomed him
into His heart,
that place of peace and love.
Lazarus was now at rest within
the Source of Life.

The rich man also died.
Because he had rejected Lazarus
and never wanted to share anything with him,
he went immediately to the place of torment.

During his lifetime,
the rich man could have come close to Lazarus.
But he did not!
He let a huge gap grow between the two of them.

Jesus says that now
there is a gap which no one can bridge
between Lazarus, in the place of peace,
and the rich man, in the place of torment.

Jesus invites us to bridge the gap
that separates us from those who are poor.
We can still do it now.
One day it will be too late!

Our world today is so divided
between those like Lazarus and the "rich."

On one side, there are those who are satisfied:
    they have money, friends, a good position.
    But often they are closed up in their own world.

        They only think of themselves.

On the other side, there are those who suffer:
    they cannot cope with life,
    they are alone, abandoned.
    They live in great insecurity.

Jesus came for all the men, all the women,
all the children of our world.
He comes to announce the Good News:
His Father loves each one of us.
He comes to tell us that our world is not
condemned to live with division, struggle, hatred,
war and death.
He calls us to greater sharing, unity and love.

He gives each one His Holy Spirit
    in order to change our hearts
    so that we may be men and women who share,
    so that we may close the gaps
    that separate people,
    so that we may work toward reconciliation.

Jesus lived simply with simple people in Nazareth.
Nobody noticed Him there, hidden as He was,
poor among the poor.

The poor were always His friends.
He loved to live with them.

Jesus came to bring light,
to open the eyes of our hearts,
to heal our blindness.

*Sometimes, Jesus shared a meal
with publicans and sinners.
He was criticized for that.
Jesus listened and spoke to women
who were caught in prostitution.
He was also criticized for that.*

Jesus touched the lepers, the "untouchables,"
    those men and women rejected by others.

He healed them.
He is close to those who suffer.

Jesus comes to announce the Good News to the poor.
To each one of us, when we feel poor,
weak or broken,

He says: "Rise up!
        You are beautiful,
        you are precious,
        and I love you!
        Go!
        You too can love,
        you can give life,
        you can also spread the Good News.
        Do not be afraid! I am with you!"

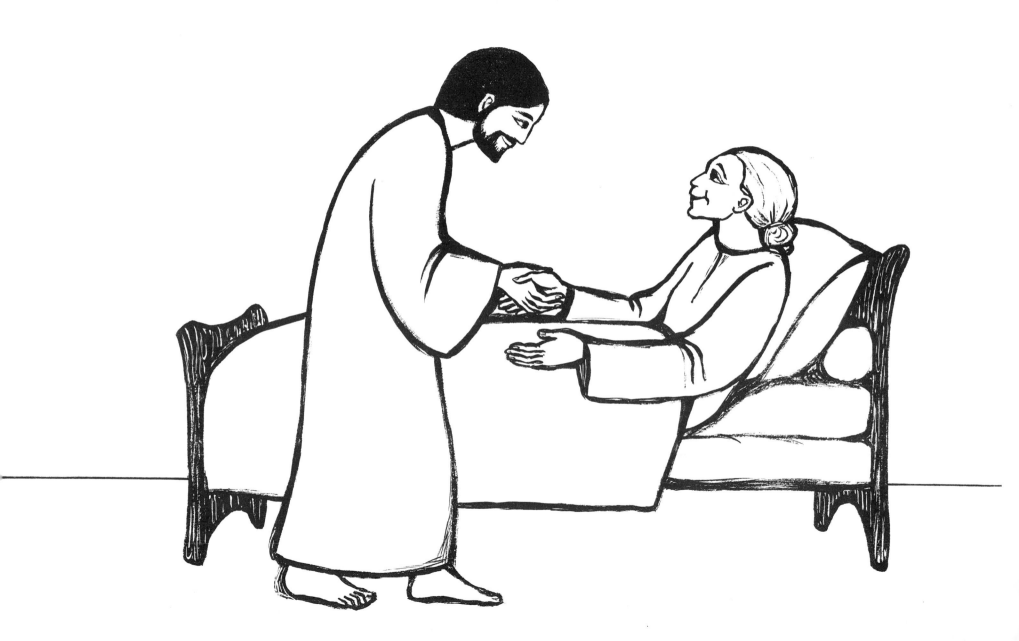

Jesus also comes to each one of us
wrapped up in our apparent riches,
        riches which hide interior poverty.

We are frightened to look at that poverty.

However He comes to open our hearts
which are often closed to the love of the Father
        and to the suffering of others.

One day, Jesus is walking
through the streets of Jericho.
There are many people there.
They all want to see Jesus.
Zacchaeus is also there.
He is a rich man but he is so small,
he cannot see Jesus in the crowd.

Luke 19, 1-10

Then Zacchaeus has a good idea.
He runs and climbs up a big tree.
Now he can see Jesus better.

When Jesus passes by, He stops
and says to Zacchaeus:
"Come down quickly,
for today I want
to come to your home."

Jesus goes and shares a meal
with Zacchaeus and his family.
In this way, He says: "I am your friend!"

Jesus says to each one of us who is rich:

"Come down from your tree,
from your pedestal!
I want to come to your home.
Open your heart; welcome Me.
You do not have to lock yourself up
in your wealth.
Do not be afraid.
I will teach you the joy of loving."

One day, another rich man asks Jesus:
    "What must I do to have eternal life?"

Jesus looks at him with love and says:
    "If you want to be perfect,
    sell all you have,
    give the money to the poor
    and follow Me."

    Jesus lives very simply and poorly.
    He invites the young man
    to become his friend
    and to live with Him.

Mark 10, 17-22

The young man does not believe
in the deep love of Jesus for him.
He does not trust Him.
He walks away from Jesus, very sad
because he is very rich
          and does not want to share.

"It is more difficult for a rich man
to enter into the Kingdom of Heaven
than for a camel to pass through the eye
of a needle," says Jesus.

Luke 18, 25

The Gospel does not say how sad Jesus was,
how His heart was hurt by the refusal
of this young man,
his lack of trust.

Jesus loves each one of us.
He wants to give us His Holy Spirit
    in order to heal us from our fears
    and selfishness,
    in order to open the doors of our hearts.

But Jesus cannot give us His Spirit,
this new force of love,
unless we really trust Him,
unless we become humble, like little children.

Only then can we grow in love.

Matthew 18, 3

When I walk with Jesus,
He always leads me to the poorest,
the lowliest and the lost,
so that I may open my heart to them.

Then, Jesus helps me discover
that He Himself is hidden in the poor:

"When I was hungry, you gave Me to eat;
when I was thirsty, you gave Me to drink."

Matthew 25, 35-40

"When I was a stranger, you welcomed Me."

"When I was sick, in prison, you visited Me. When I was naked, you clothed Me."

"Whatever you do to the least of My brothers, you do to Me."

Yes it is such a mystery!
Each time I am kind and loving
to someone in distress,
I do it to Jesus.
He looks at me and says: "Thank you!
I love you."

At another time, Jesus says:

"He who welcomes one of these little ones
in My name welcomes Me.
And he who welcomes Me,
welcomes the One who sent Me."

Who can believe that Jesus and His Father
are hidden in this person who is completely broken,
or in this child who is deeply wounded?

Luke 9, 48

To welcome the poor means
to become their friend,
to live a heart to heart relationship with them,
to listen to them, to touch them with respect,
to discover their beauty,
and reveal this beauty to them,
to love them just as they are.

To open our hearts to the poor
is to open our hearts to Jesus!

It is not always easy for me
to be close to someone in anguish,
to enter into a heart to heart relationship
with him.
It is much easier to do something for him,
to give from a distance.

When I try to welcome that person,
to listen to him,
to become his friend,

I discover my own incapacity to love
and all the harshness and selfishness
in my heart.
I discover my own fears, wounds and hypocrisy.
I discover that I too am poor!

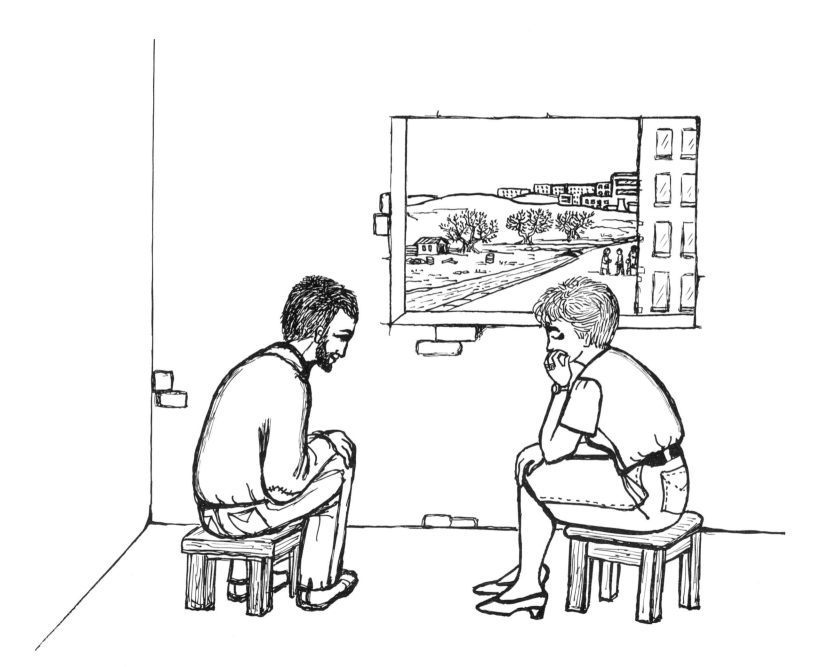

Jesus is not only hidden in the poor,
        in those who are hungry or in prison,

He is also hidden in me, in my own poverty.

When I try to follow Jesus,
I seek to serve the poor.
But I discover also that I am the poor.
Then I see how much I need Jesus
to give me strength and courage.

He tells me: "My grace is sufficient.
        Do not be afraid. I am with you."

The world cannot cope with poverty.

We tend to ignore or deny our limits,
our fragility, our vulnerability
and incapacity to love.

But when I walk with Jesus,
He helps me to be myself,
to accept myself just as I am,
with my weakness and my strength.

Like a child, I put my hand in His hand.
I let Him guide me.
I learn how to give life to others.

When I walk with Jesus,
when I recognize Him,
there is a deep joy in my heart,
    as in the hearts of the disciples of Emmaus.

He teaches me not to walk away from suffering,
but rather to see His presence
in the heart of suffering.
He invites me to touch His wounds, like Thomas,
    and to discover that resurrection flows
        from His wounds and His cross.

Then I cry out: "My Lord and my God!"

John 20, 24-28

Jesus suffered a great deal in His life.
He wept in the Garden of Gethsemani.
He was abandoned by all His friends.
He was condemned to death.

He was put in prison, tortured and scourged.
They pushed a crown of thorns on His head.
He carried a heavy cross on His back.

Yet, Jesus was the Innocent One.
He came to announce the Good News to the poor,
   to liberate hearts from all kinds of slavery,
   to comfort and heal,
   to love.

Nevertheless, He was nailed to a cross.
He died praying: "Father, into Your hands
                  I commend My Spirit."

When the Jews celebrated Passover,
they sacrificed a lamb to God.
They offered up to God the very best.
The blood of the lamb was shed on the altar.
Then, they ate the lamb.
This offering was an act of adoration and thanksgiving
for all God had done for them.

Jesus is the "Lamb of God,"
sacrificed and offered to the Father
on the altar of the cross
in order to save all men, women and children.

"Lamb of God who takes away the sins
of the world,
have mercy on us!"

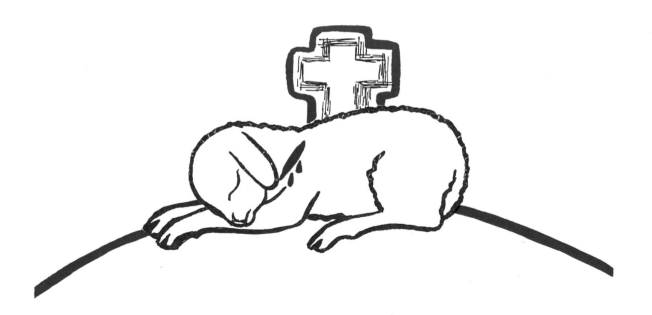

Jesus reveals to us the secret hidden
in suffering:
through His wounds, He saves us,
through His death, He gives us life,
through His resurrection,
            we rise up
            and become men and women of hope!

At the Eucharist, we relive the mystery
of the sacrifice of Jesus on the cross.
Jesus offers Himself to the Father
in the form of bread and wine.
The bread becomes His Body, the wine His Blood
for the forgiveness of sins.

He renews His covenant with us.
We live from His resurrection
and we wait for His return in glory.

Jesus says to His apostles:
"This is My Body given up for you.
Take and eat it.
This is the cup of My Blood.
Take and drink it.
Do this in memory of Me."

He says to each one of us: "He who eats My Body
and drinks My Blood
lives in Me and I in him."

The Body of Jesus is a tremendous gift.
He is truly present in the Eucharist!

Luke 22, 19-20 / John 6, 56

When we go to Communion,
> we live in communion with the sufferings
> of Jesus;
> we live in communion with the sufferings
> of our world.

With Jesus, and with all those who suffer,
> we offer our lives
> for the salvation of the world.

We receive His life so that we can live
in the hope of the resurrection.

There is an intimate link
       between Jesus present in the Eucharist and
       Jesus present in the poorest and the weakest.

They help us discover Jesus in the Eucharist.
And when we receive the Body of Jesus,
He opens our eyes and hearts to His presence
in the poor.

At the cross, Mary was present.
She loved Jesus so much.
She lived for Him.
She offered her life to the Father with Him.
She is the silent woman,
      a woman of compassion.

She teaches me how to be compassionate,
      to comfort the afflicted,
      to suffer with them,
      to love them,
      to have hope.

Jesus and Mary help us discover
the meaning of our sufferings,
how to offer them up to the Father.
Through this offering of love,
        we also live the cross and the resurrection.

In this way, we can also bring much love
into our world.
We can give life.

The two disciples on the road to Emmaus
are walking away from their community.
They are discouraged and feeling terribly alone.
They have lost confidence in Jesus
and in their community.
But once they recognize Jesus
and discover that He is alive,
                    they quickly go back to their
                    community.

They have found new hope!

When I walk with Jesus,
He gives me brothers and sisters.
He gives me a community.
He binds us together.

There is a covenant between us:
 "Where two or three are gathered in My name,
 I am in their midst," says Jesus.

Some people may be very alone
but they are never all alone.
In a hidden way, they are linked
to other brothers and sisters in the Church.

Matthew 18, 20

Jesus lived in a community.
He was born into a family.
Mary is His Mother.
Joseph loved Him with the heart of a father.
Jesus, Mary and Joseph lived together
for many years.
They were the first Christian community.

Jesus, Mary and Joseph loved each other very much.
They served each other.
They worked together.
They prayed to the Father together.
They shared their joy together.
They were ONE
as the Father, Son and Holy Spirit are ONE.
Their community was a source of life where many
poor people came to draw strength and peace.

Jesus created a community with His disciples.
He called each one of them by his name.
He asked each one to walk with Him,
and to build community together.

The night before He died,
He said to them: "Love one another
as I have loved you."

And He prayed: "Father, that they may be ONE
even as we are One,
I in them, and You in Me
that they may be perfectly ONE."

John 13, 34
John 17, 22-23

Just before He died on the cross,
Jesus created a covenant of love
between Mary and John.
He said to Mary, indicating John:
    "Woman, here is your son."

He said to John:
    "Here is your mother."

And from that moment on,
John and Mary belonged to each other.

John 19, 25-28

On the feast of Pentecost, the Father and Jesus
sent the Holy Spirit to the disciples
    gathered together in prayer with Mary.

The community of the Church was born
with all its diversity of cultures and languages!

Jesus and the Holy Spirit sent the disciples
throughout the world to announce the Word of God,
to baptize in the name of the Father, Son and Holy Spirit,
to create communities founded in the name of Jesus.

Jesus is present in His Church.

He says to Peter:

"You are Peter
and on this rock I will build My Church,
and the powers of death shall not prevail against it.
I will give you the keys of the Kingdom.
Whatever you bind on earth, shall be bound in Heaven,
and whatever you loose on earth,
shall be loosed in Heaven."

He gives Peter the keys to the Kingdom.

Matthew 16, 18-21

Jesus is the Eternal Word of the Father.
His Word is the Word of God.
His Word gives life.

It nourishes and strengthens our minds and hearts.
It is a promise that is given, a path to follow.
It brings the fullness of truth.

When a disciple speaks of Jesus and His Gospel
with faith and love,
Jesus is present in those words.
When we listen, our hearts begin to burn within.

"He who listens to you
listens to Me," says Jesus.

Luke 10, 16

The Bible is the Word of God.
It tells us the Sacred History of humanity.
Mary received it and kept it in her heart.
If we read it with love,
if we receive it and keep it in our hearts
   as a message from the Father to His children,

then we will grow like Jesus in love and wisdom.

The Word of God is a light of love which nourishes
our faith, our minds and our hearts.
It is a Word which accomplishes what it says.

Throughout the years,
ever since that feast of Pentecost,
the Church has continually announced
the living Word
so that hearts may continue to burn within
and open up to the Spirit of God.

Often, we need a man or woman of God
to help us read and understand the Word,
to recognize the "sacred history"
of our own lives,
to discern the Word of God for each moment
of our lives.

There are different types of communities.

There is the community of the family,
    man and woman united in marriage.

Jesus creates a covenant between them.
The heart of the man is given to his wife.
The heart of the woman is given to her husband.
This union is a sacrament,
a place where God is truly present.

Through the sacrament of marriage,
through the promise of God
and the love that flows from Him,
a man and woman can continue to love each other
until the end of their lives.
They are a sign of the love of the Holy Trinity.

This covenant between man and woman in marriage
is fruitful.
Their fecundity is also a sign of the Holy Trinity.
Living as husband and wife, they give life,
they communicate love and hope.

As parents they are called to serve
their children,
> to help them grow,
> become free, loving and faithful.

Jesus gives to parents a love
that is not possessive
> but liberating,
> life-giving.

Family life is not always easy.
A man can flee relationship in work
and distractions.
He can become difficult with his wife
and children,
no longer communicating with them.
He becomes less attentive, less loving.
A woman can become aggressive.
She too can flee relationship in work
and can lose a sense of service and love.
Thus a wall is built up between them.
They need the grace of the Holy Spirit
         and hearts that are continually being renewed
so that their love can deepen
and that their union be founded on welcoming
the other just as she or he is
and on forgiveness 70 × 7 times!

Matthew 18, 22

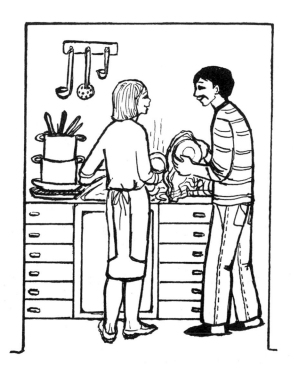

Jesus calls some people to live a covenant
between them in community life.
They belong to one another.
They are a sign of God's tenderness
and faithfulness.
Some are called to live celibacy.
They receive this as a gift from Jesus
        which is a source of life for others.

Jesus invites us to live community.
It is a place of healing
where people can grow in covenant,
commitment to others and openness to the world.
There are communities where people live together.
There are others
where people come together regularly
for times of prayer, sharing and service to others.

Community life is not always easy.
In the community,
there are some people I really like!

  We have the same sensitivity
  and see things the same way.
  We are a source of life and strength
  for each other.

But there are others I just can't stand!

  We never agree but get on each other's nerves.
  There is a block between us.

We need Jesus and the gift of His Holy Spirit
in order to be able to accept and love each person
in the way Jesus loves him or her.

Each community, like the Church, is a body.
In this body, each member is different:
  each one has his or her gift,
  each one is important.

In this body, the weaker, more suffering,
more broken ones have a very special place.

Jesus continually invites me to serve
especially the poorest,
  the lowliest,
  the lonely.

In the community,
some are called to be like Martha,
others like Mary.
Martha works hard; she serves Jesus.
Mary sits at His feet, listens to Him.
Jesus loves both Martha and Mary;
both are important.
Martha should not get upset with Mary
or judge her.
They need each other.

Luke 10, 38-42

At the head of community, there is a leader,
a shepherd.
The shepherd is essentially a servant.
Mothers and fathers are shepherds
to their children.
Educators and teachers are shepherds.
Priests, ministers, bishops and the Pope
are shepherds too.

Jesus showed us how to exercise our shepherdhood
  by washing the feet of His disciples.

John 13, 1-18

"Which is greater, the one who sits at table or
the one who serves.
Is it not the one who is served?
I am among you as one who serves."

Luke 22,27

Shepherds have a very important role to play.
They walk at the head of their people;
they show the way.
They know each one by his or her name.
They listen and are attentive to their needs.
They help each one find his or her place
and grow in truth.
They are guardians of unity.

John 10

There are good shepherds:
>   they lay down their lives for their sheep.
>   They sacrifice their own personal interests
>   in order to really serve others.

There are bad shepherds:
>   they seek privileges and power;
>   they do not listen to their flock.

When the wolf comes
or when there are other dangers,
they run away because they do not really care
for their people.

It is difficult to be a good shepherd.
He or she is never perfect
but has limits and faults.
Shepherds need to be helped and loved
in order to exercise their gift.
Jesus invites us
to be humble and obedient to each other.
Each one of us is called to recognize and
love authority and the gift of each person.

Every community is based on trust,
      trust that it is Jesus who calls us together;
      trust in one another,
      that we are all brothers and sisters,
      that each one has a place and can grow.

Yes, Jesus is alive today.
I recognize Him
   in the community of brothers and sisters,
   in the covenant that binds us together.

A community founded on Jesus is not a ghetto.
It is not a stagnant pond
but rather a spring of living water.
It is alive, open and welcoming!
It gives life to others,
especially to those who are neglected and lonely.

A community founded on Jesus is a source of
abundant life for others.

When a community becomes rich,
it tends to build walls around itself,
to protect itself.
There is fear.

When a community is poor,
it has nothing to defend;
it knows that God watches over and protects it.
It is a place of welcome and trust.

"Look at the birds of the air;
they neither sow nor reap nor gather in barns,
and yet your heavenly Father feeds them.
Are you not of more value than they?

Therefore do not be anxious, saying:
    'What shall we eat?' or 'What shall we drink?'
    or 'What shall we wear?'

For the Gentiles seek all these things;
and your heavenly Father knows
that you need them all.
Seek first the Kingdom of God
and all these things shall be yours as well.
Do not be anxious about tomorrow,
for tomorrow will be anxious for itself.
Let each day's own trouble be sufficient
for the day."

Matthew 6, 26-34

Communities founded on the love of Jesus
open their doors wide to receive
the poor and the lonely.
Jesus teaches us to give with confidence:

> *"Behold I stand at the door and I knock.*
> *If anyone hears My voice*
> *and opens the door to Me,*
> *I will come in to him*
> *and will eat with him, and he with Me."*

Revelation 3, 20

Some people live on prayer.
You find them in monasteries
but also in prisons and hospitals.
Sometimes they are bedridden or in wheelchairs,
or sometimes they are old, sick, and lonely.
They have time.
All day long
they remain close to the heart of Jesus
in prayer and love.
They remain quietly there, offering all the pain,
violence and injustice of our world.

They are like Mary, interceding for the world.
Their fecundity is tremendous!
They are like hidden springs
which irrigate the earth.

Forgiveness is one of the greatest gifts
of the Father to humanity.

So quickly I can hurt another person:
    I do not allow him or her to be different.
    I do not really listen.
    I just close myself up in my own needs
    and problems.

To forgive means to break down the barriers
which separate people.
To forgive means to be an instrument of peace.
To forgive means to rediscover the covenant
that binds us together.

I have turned away
from Jesus who is the source of life.
I have turned away from Him in the poorest
and the weakest of my brothers and sisters.
I let myself be seduced by wealth and pleasure.
I wanted to prove that I was better than others.
I was closed up in my own sadness and despair.
I set up barriers around me.

That doesn't matter!
If I come back to Jesus, He forgives me.
He opens His heart to me and thus opens my heart
to my brothers and sisters.

There is such guilt in our hearts.
We need forgiveness
and a concrete sign of God's forgiveness.
Jesus sends us His priests who tell us:
"I forgive you, in the name of the Father,
the Son and the Holy Spirit."
After His resurrection,
Jesus says to His disciples:
"Receive the Holy Spirit.
Whose sins you shall forgive,
they are forgiven;
and whose sins you shall retain,
they are retained."
The sacrament of reconciliation is vital
for growth in love.

John 20, 22-23

Jesus invites me to forgive as He forgives.
He invites me to become a man or woman
of forgiveness.

To forgive is to welcome and carry the weakness
of another.
It is to recognize the covenant that binds us.
It is to have a heart full of kindness
and compassion.
It is to pray
for those who reject, persecute and torture.

"Father, forgive them for they know not
what they do."

Luke 23, 34

At the heart of the message of Jesus,
there is forgiveness and love of our enemies.

"But I tell you, love your enemies.
Do good to those who hate you.
Bless those who curse you.
Pray for those who persecute you."

There are enemies outside of the community;
they try to destroy us.
There are enemies within the community;
they frighten us.
We can no longer talk to each other.

Jesus invites us to love our enemies.
If we are alone, this is impossible.
We need the Spirit that Jesus promises us.
He gradually takes away from my heart
all fear, bitterness and hatred.

Luke 6, 27-28

Celebration is at the heart of community.
To celebrate means to give thanks,
to express our joy and our trust,
because Jesus has freed us from our prison
of loneliness.

He has come to be with us.
He gives us to each other;
He creates a covenant between us.
We will never again be alone.
We belong to a people that is united and loved.

In our world
there is so much suffering and anguish.
In each one of us
there is love, but there is also hatred and fear.

But Jesus is alive!
He forgives us; He guides us.
He helps us carry each other's burdens.
And so let us celebrate.
With all our heart and in truth,
we can sing: "Our Father."

Each meal is meant to be a celebration,
a celebration of our covenant.
There are special meals on feast days.

Jesus tells us that the Kingdom of Heaven
is like a wedding feast!
He himself was present at the wedding of Cana.

Jesus also tells us: "When you have a celebration,
invite the poor, the lame
and the blind."

It is with them that we experience true celebration.
He gave us the gift of His Body and Blood
during His last meal with the disciples.
The Eucharist is the most beautiful of all
celebrations!

Luke 14, 12

Each encounter with another person can be
a celebration.
We open up our hearts to each other.
We live a communion of love with one another.
There is a presence of God,
a presence of the Holy Trinity.

Jesus loved to pray in the silence of His heart.
He loved His Father so much.
Everything Jesus is comes from Father.
Jesus is in the bosom of the Father,
His Perfect Image,
His Beloved Son.

This communion with the Father was the source
of His whole life.

He invites us also to pray in the silence
of our hearts.
Prayer is an encounter
with the Father, the Son and the Holy Spirit.
It is the most beautiful of all encounters;
it is truly a celebration.

To pray is to put ourselves before the Father
in complete trust, like a child.
Thus prayer is adoration.

Adoration can take on many forms:

> a song of praise: "Blessed are You, Father!"

> a cry: "Come! The world needs You so much!"

> a rest: "Let me live in Your love."

> an offering: "Father, I give You my life,
> all that is beautiful,
> all that is wounded,
> all that hurts,
> for my brothers and sisters
> throughout the world!"

> Thus, it is sacrifice.

If we are people who pray,
if our communities are living, loving,
close to the poor,
we will be witnesses of Jesus in society
and at work.
We will help break down the barriers that separate
countries, peoples, classes.
We will become real instruments of peace
and reconciliation.
We will work toward a better world
where all men, women and children,
even the smallest and the most helpless,
can live their human dignity as children of God
in a loving community.

There is hope!

Yes, Jesus says to us:

"Be not afraid
for I am with you always
until the end of time!"

Matthew 28, 20